NOVELLO C[...]

SHOWTU[...]ES

DOTS
The Camden Music Shop

*132 St. Pancras Way,
London NW1 9NB*

Tel: 020-7482-5424
Fax: 020-7482-5434
E-mail: dot@dotsonline.co.uk
Web: www.dotsonline.co.uk

6.95

Novello
part of The Music Sales Group
London / New York / Paris / Sydney / Copenhagen / Berlin / Madrid / Hong Kong / Tokyo

Published by

Novello Publishing Limited
part of The Music Sales Group
14-15 Berners Street, London W1T 3LJ, UK.

Exclusive Distributors:

Music Sales Limited
Distribution Centre, Newmarket Road,
Bury St Edmunds, Suffolk IP33 3YB, UK.

Music Sales Pty Limited
Units 3-4, 17 Willfox Street, Condell Park
NSW 2200, Australia.

Order No. NOV164406
ISBN 978-1-78305-443-5

Edited by Ruth Power.
Music processed by Paul Ewers Music Design.

Printed in the EU.

NOVELLO CHORAL
SHOWTUNES

**THIS CHORAL POPS COLLECTION MAKES A GREAT INTRODUCTION
TO THE WORLD OF MUSICAL THEATRE FOR THE AMATEUR CHOIR
WITH FAVOURITE SHOW SONGS FROM THE PAST FIVE DECADES.**

BRING HIM HOME

MUSIC BY CLAUDE-MICHEL SCHÖNBERG
LYRICS BY ALAIN BOUBLIL & HERBERT KRETZMER

Arranged by Francis Shaw

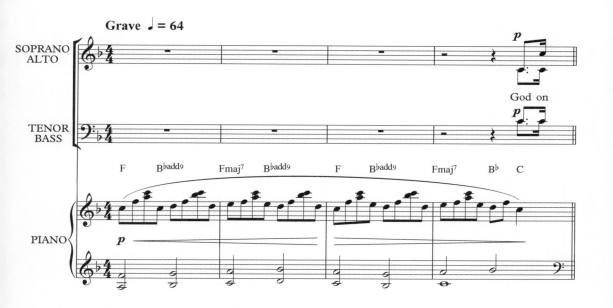

5

8

9

ALL I ASK OF YOU

MUSIC BY ANDREW LLOYD WEBBER, LYRICS BY CHARLES HART
ADDITIONAL LYRICS BY RICHARD STILGOE

Arranged by Barrie Carson Turner

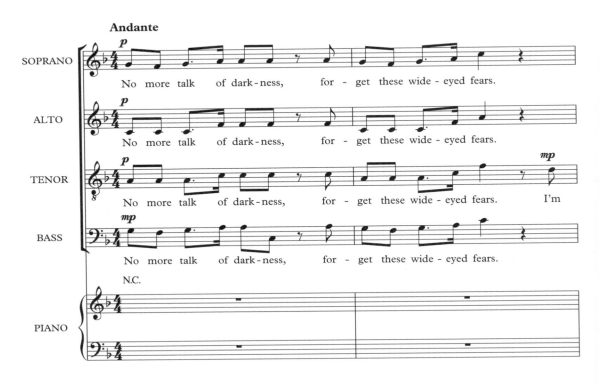

Say you love me ev-'ry wak - ing mo - ment,
Say you love me ev-'ry wak - ing mo - ment,
Say you love me ev-'ry wak - ing mo - ment,
Say you love me ev-'ry wak - ing mo - ment,

Fadd9   Dm7   Gm7   C11

turn my head with talk of sum-mer-time._
turn my head with talk of sum-mer-time._
turn my head with talk of sum-mer-time._
turn my head with talk of sum-mer-time._

div.

F/A   Dm7   Gm7   C11

Say you need me with you now and al-ways;

unis.
Say you need me with you now and al-ways;

Say you need me with you now and al-ways;

Say you need me with you now and al-ways;

Fadd⁹   Dm⁷   Gm⁷   C¹¹

rit.

mf   *div.* *dim.*
pro-mise me that all you say is true, that's all I ask of

mf
pro-mise me all you say is true.

mf
pro-mise me all you say is true.

mf
pro-mise me all you say is true.

F/A   B♭   F/C   C¹¹   C⁷

a tempo

Say you'll share with me one love, one life - time;

Say you'll share share one love, share one life - time;

you. Say you'll share share one love, share one life - time;

Say you'll share share one love, share one life - time;

Fadd⁹   Dm⁷   Gm⁷   C¹¹

say the word and I will fol-low you.___

say the word and I will fol-low you.___

say the word and I will fol-low you.___

say the word and I will fol-low you.___

F/A   Dm⁷   Gm⁷   C¹¹

21

BIG SPENDER

WORDS BY DOROTHY FIELDS, MUSIC BY CY COLEMAN

Arranged by Nicholas Hare

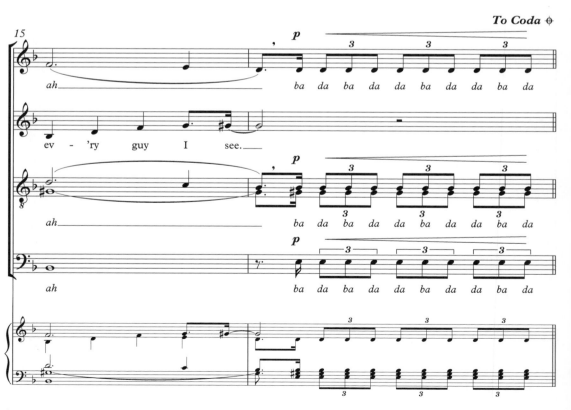

⊕ *Coda*

29

I HAVE A DREAM

WORDS & MUSIC BY BENNY ANDERSSON & BJÖRN ULVAEUS

Arranged by Quentin Thomas

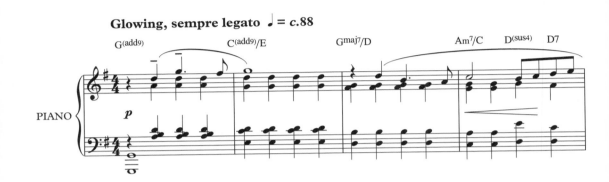

32

ev - 'ry-thing I see. I be-lieve in an - -

ev - 'ry - thing. I be-lieve in an - -

ev - 'ry-thing I see. I be-lieve in

ev - 'ry-thing I see. I be-lieve in

B(sus4)   Bm⁷   C(add9)   D/C   D   N.C.

- gels. When I know the time is right for me, I'll cross the

- gels. When I know the time is right for me.

an - gels. When the time is right for me.

an - gels. When I know the time is right for me.

stream, _____ I have a dream. _____
I'll _____ cross _____ the _____ stream, I have a dream. _____
I'll _____ cross _____ the _____ stream, I have a dream. _____
I'll _____ cross _____ the _____ stream, I have a dream. _____

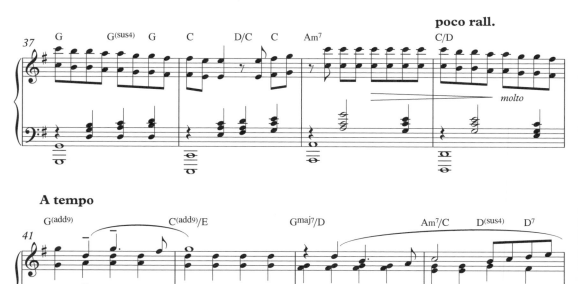

35

37

THE LAST NIGHT OF THE WORLD

MUSIC BY CLAUDE-MICHEL SCHÖNBERG
LYRICS BY RICHARD MALTBY JR. & ALAIN BOUBLIL
ADAPTED FROM ORIGINAL FRENCH LYRICS BY ALAIN BOUBLIL

Arranged by Francis Shaw

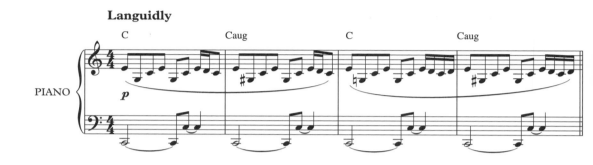

change, when to - mor - row comes,

Our lives will change, when to - mor - row comes,

To - night our

To-night our hearts drown the dis - tant drums,

and we have

and we have

hearts drown the dis - tant drums,

Dm

Dm/C

B♭

stacc.

41

42

48

Played on a so - lo sax - o - phone. __

Played on a so - lo sax - o - phone. __

Played on a so - lo sax - o - phone. __

Played on a so - lo sax - o - phone. __

ENJOYED THIS BOOK?

Whether you want to be the next musical *Star of Stage or Screen*, or you just love singing along to your favourite shows... why not check out these fantastic titles...

...available now, these books come complete with PIANO/VOCAL/GUITAR arrangements, FULL LYRICS and superb 'soundalike' BACKING TRACKS on CD

A selection of 12 of the most memorable songs from the hit musical **Mamma Mia!** Including...

Dancing Queen
Knowing Me, Knowing You
Mamma Mia
Money, Money, Money
The Name Of The Game
One Of Us
S.O.S.
Super Trouper
Take A Chance On Me
Thank You For The Music
Voulez-Vous
The Winner Takes It All

This book is about Freedom, Beauty, Truth, Love and above all else... contains a great selection of FABULOUS songs & medleys from **Moulin Rouge!** Including...

Children Of The Revolution
Come What May
Complainte De La Butte
El Tango De Roxanne
Elephant Love Medley
Lady Marmalade
Nature Boy
One Day I'll Fly Away
Rhythm Of The Night
Sparkling Diamonds
Your Song

These titles, plus many more, are available from your local Music Retailer.
In case of difficulty, visit www.musicsales.com or email marketing@musicsales.co.uk